WEIRD BUT TRUE SCIENCE

Weird But True Space Facts

Carmen Bredeson

Series Science Consultant:
Mary Poulson, PhD
Central Washington University
Ellensburg, WA

Series Literacy Consultant:
Allan A. De Fina, PhD
Dean, College of Education/Professor of Literacy Education
New Jersey City University
Past President of the New Jersey Reading Association

CONTENTS

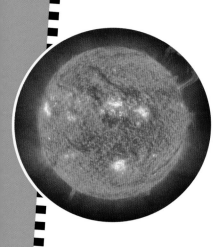

WORDS TO KNOW

lava **[LAH vuh]**—Melted rock that comes out of a volcano.

meteor **[MEE tee ur]**—A space rock burning in Earth's atmosphere.

plutoid **[PLOO toyd]**—An icy round object in space that goes around the Sun. It is very far out in space, past Neptune. Pluto, which used to be a planet, is now a plutoid. A plutoid can also be called an icy dwarf planet.

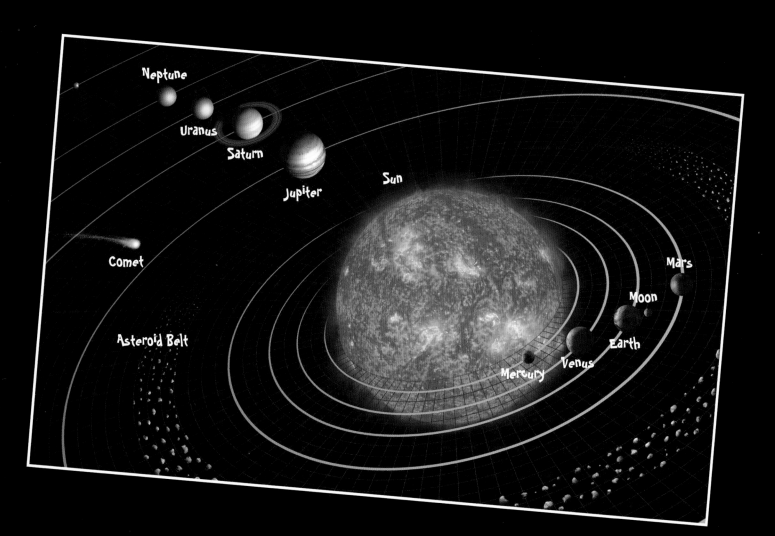

WEIRD SPACE

Did you know that the sky in space is black?
Or that giant space rocks have crashed into Earth?
Come along on a wild ride and learn some weird
things about space!

GAS PLANETS
HELP! I'M FALLING . . .

Jupiter, Saturn, Uranus, and Neptune are called gas giants. They do not have solid ground like Earth. They are made of gas. You could not stand on the gas giants. It would be like trying to stand on a cloud.

It's weird, but it's true!

Jupiter

Neptune

Uranus

Saturn

This art shows the surface of the giant gas planet Jupiter. A spacecraft is coming to study the planet.

MOON FOOTPRINTS
Doesn't anyone sweep up here?

There are footprints on the Moon. They have been there a LONG time. Astronauts left the prints about forty years ago. The Moon has no wind to blow them away. There is no rain to wash them away.

It's weird, but it's true!

BERRINGER METEOR CRATER
Watch out below!

A **meteor** blazed across Earth's sky 50,000 years ago. The giant space rock was bigger than a football field. It crashed into the ground. It left a hole about one mile wide. You can still see the big crater in Arizona.

It's weird, but it's true!

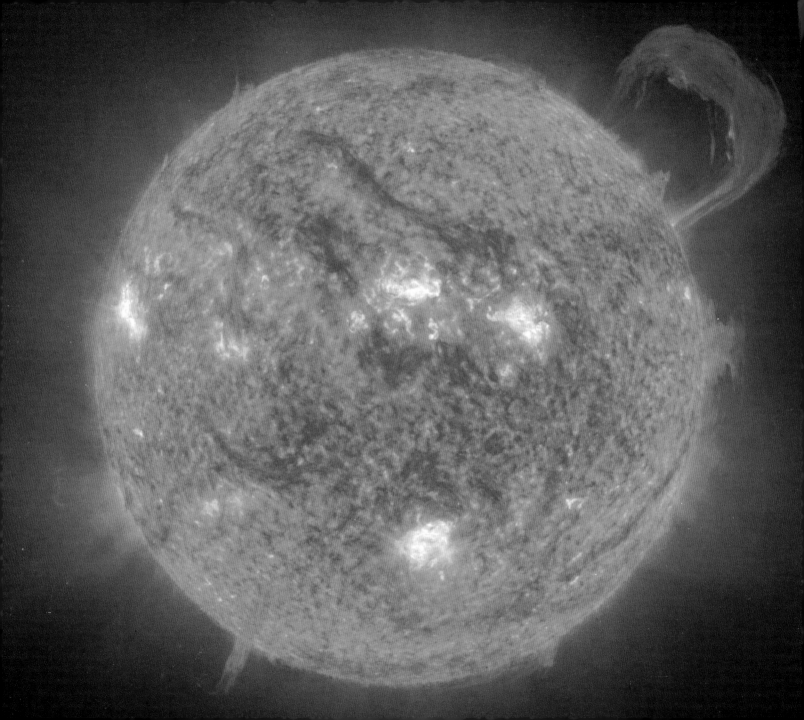

THE SUN
A shining giant

The Sun is a big star, but do you know how big? A MILLION Earths could fit inside the Sun! It is the biggest thing in our solar system. Some stars in the universe are even bigger. But they are far away and look very small to us.

It's weird, but it's true!

This drawing shows how the Sun is so much bigger than the eight planets.

Ida the Asteroid
Space rocks!

Asteroids are rocks that look like huge potatoes.
Some asteroids are bigger than a mountain.
Ida has its own little moon, called Dactyl.
Dactyl goes around and around Ida far out in space.

It's weird, but it's true!

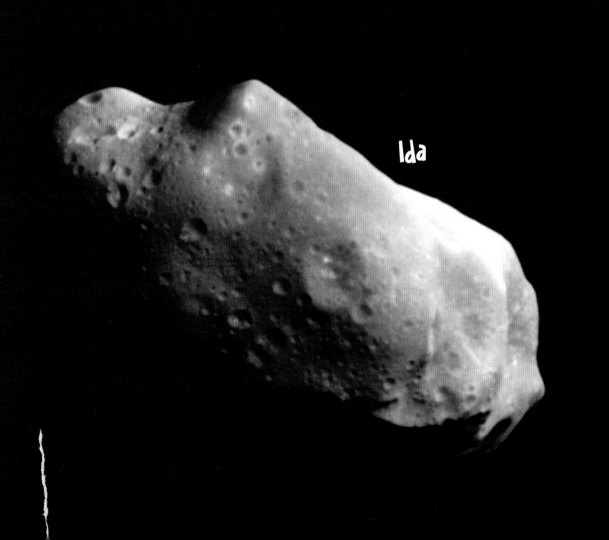

Ida

Dactyl

Our Moon
Lakes of lava

What made the dark areas on the moon? **Lava**! Long ago, lava shot out of volcanoes on the Moon. It flowed across the ground and ran into low spots. The lava got hard. Some people think the dark areas look like a face. What do you see?

It's weird, but it's true!

SPACE
Is it day or night?

The sky is black in space, ALL of the time. Why?
On Earth, sunlight passes through the air around
our planet. The air bends the light. It lets us see color.
There is no air in space to bend the light. So, the sky is
always black.

It's weird, but it's true!

KUIPER BELT
Can it hold up your pants?

The Kuiper (KY pur) Belt is an area way out in space, past Neptune. The Kuiper Belt is full of big chunks of rocks called **plutoids**. Scientists look for new plutoids. They found one that is even bigger than the dwarf planet Pluto!

It's weird, but it's true!

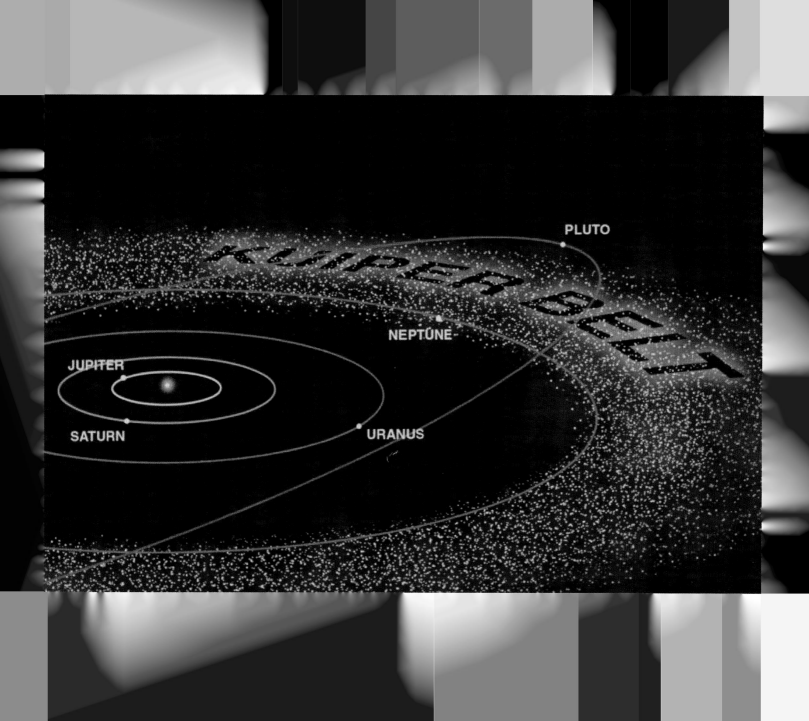

LEARN MORE

Books

Bailey, Jacqui. *Up, Down, All Around: A Story of Gravity*. Minneapolis: Picture Window Books, 2006.

Carson, Mary Kay. *Extreme Planets! Q&A*. New York: Harper Collins, 2008.

Howard, Fran. *The Kuiper Belt*. Edina, Minn.: ABDO Publishing Company, 2008.

Riley, Peter. *Earth, Moon & Sun*. Mankato, Minn.: Smart Apple Media, 2008.

LEARN MORE

Web Sites

NASA Kids' Club
www.nasa.gov/audience/forkids/kidsclub/flash/index.html

The Space Place
http://spaceplace.jpl.nasa.gov/en/kids/

Your Weight on Other Worlds
www.exploratorium.edu/ronh/weight/index.html

Index

To our wonderful grandchildren: Andrew, Charlie, Kate, and Caroline

Enslow Elementary, an imprint of Enslow Publishers, Inc.

Enslow Elementary® is a registered trademark of Enslow Publishers, Inc.

Library of Congress Cataloging-in-Publication Data

Bredeson, Carmen.
   Weird but true space facts / Carmen Bredeson.
      p. cm. — (Weird but true science)
   Includes index.
   Summary: "Find out about gravity, the asteroid ida, the berringer meteor crater, the moon, and other weird space facts"—Provided by publisher.
   ISBN 978-0-7660-3863-9
   1. Astronomy—Miscellanea—Juvenile literature. I. Title.
   QB46.B83 2011
   520—dc22
                                          2010035877

Paperback ISBN 978-1-59845-371-3
Printed in China
052011 Leo Paper Group, Heshan City, Guangdong, China

10 9 8 7 6 5 4 3 2 1

To Our Readers: We have done our best to make sure all Internet Addresses in this book were active and appropriate when we went to press. However, the author and the publisher have no control over and assume no liability for the material available on those Internet sites or on other Web sites they may link to. Any comments or suggestions can be sent by e-mail to comments@enslow.com or to the address on the back cover.

Photo Credits: Lunar and Planetary Institute, NASA, p. 6; NASA, pp. 1, 2, 3 (meteor), 4, 7, 8, 9, 12, 15, 19, 21; R. Hurt (SSC-Caltech), JPL-Caltech, NASA, p. 3 (plutoid); Shutterstock.com, pp. 3 (lava), 11, 16, 17, 18; SPL/Photo Researchers, Inc., p. 13.
Cover Photo: NASA

Note to Parents and Teachers: The *Weird But True Science* series supports the National Science Education Standards for K–4 science. The Words to Know section introduces subject-specific vocabulary words, including pronunciation and definitions. Early readers may need help with these new words.

Enslow Elementary
an imprint of
Enslow Publishers, Inc.
40 Industrial Road
Box 398
Berkeley Heights, NJ 07922
USA
http://www.enslow.com